Gettysburg

Frederick Tilberg

Vij Books India Pvt Ltd

New Delhi (India)

Published by

Vij Books India Pvt Ltd
(Publishers, Distributors & Importers)
2/19, Ansari Road
Delhi – 110 002
Phones: 91-11-43596460, Mob: 98110 94883
e-mail: contact@vijpublishing.com
web: www.vijbooks.in

ISBN: 978-93-93499-63-9

Contents

The field of Pickett's Charge, with his attack on the Union position at The Angle in the foreground. From the Philippoteaux painting in the Gettysburg Cyclorama.

On the gently rolling farm lands surrounding the little town of Gettysburg, Pa., was fought one of the great decisive battles of American history. For 3 days, from July 1 to 3, 1863, a gigantic struggle between 75,000 Confederates and 88,000 Union troops raged about the town and left 51,000 casualties in its wake. Heroic deeds were numerous on both sides, climaxed by the famed Confederate assault on July 3 which has become known throughout the world as Pickett's Charge. The Union victory gained on these fields ended the last Confederate invasion of the North and marked the beginning of a gradual decline in Southern military power.

Here also, a few months after the battle, Abraham Lincoln delivered his classic Gettysburg Address at the dedication of the national cemetery set apart as a burial ground for the soldiers who died in the conflict.

The Situation, Spring 1863

The situation in which the Confederacy found itself in the late spring of 1863 called for decisive action. The Union and Confederate armies had faced each other on the Rappahannock River, near Fredericksburg, Va., for 6 months. The Confederate Army of Northern Virginia, commanded by Gen. R. E. Lee, had defeated the Union forces at Fredericksburg in December 1862 and again at Chancellorsville in May 1863, but the nature of the ground gave Lee little opportunity to follow up his advantage. When he began moving his army westward, on June 3, he hoped, at least, to draw his opponent away from the river to a more advantageous battleground. At most, he might carry the war into northern territory, where supplies could be taken from the enemy and a victory could be fully exploited. Even a fairly narrow margin of victory might enable Lee to capture one or more key cities and perhaps increase northern demands for a negotiated peace.

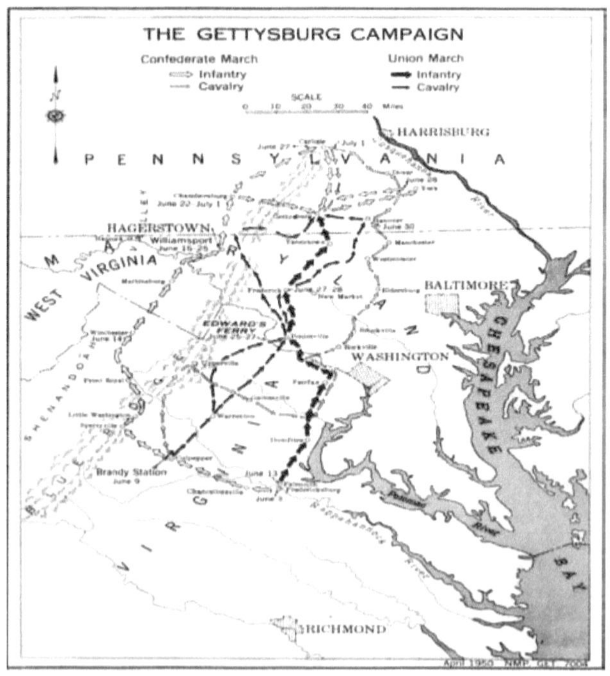

THE GETTYSBURG CAMPAIGN

**Maj. Gen. George Gordon Meade,
Commander of the Union Forces at Gettysburg.**
Courtesy National Archives.

**Gen. Robert E. Lee,
Commander of the Confederate Army at Gettysburg.**
Courtesy National Archives.

Confederate strategists had considered sending aid from Lee's army to Vicksburg, which Grant was then besieging, or dispatching help to General Bragg for his campaign against Rosecrans in Tennessee. They concluded, however, that Vicksburg could hold out until climatic conditions would force Grant to withdraw, and they reasoned that the eastern campaign was more important than that of Tennessee.

Both Union and Confederate governments had bitter opponents at home. Southern generals, reading in Northern newspapers the clamors for peace, had reason to believe that their foe's morale was fast weakening. They felt that the Army of Northern Virginia would continue to demonstrate its superiority over the Union Army of the Potomac and that the relief from constant campaigning on their own soil would have a happy effect on Southern spirit. Events were to prove, however, that the chief result of the intense alarm created by the invasion was to rally the populace to better support of the Union government.

Statue of General Meade, located on Cemetery Ridge.

The Virginia Memorial, surmounted by the statue of
General Lee, on Seminary Ridge.

Gettysburg, as it appeared from Seminary Ridge a
short time after the battle. (Brady photograph.)

The Plan of Campaign

Lee's plan of campaign was undoubtedly similar to that of his invasion which ended in the battle of Antietam in September 1862. He then called attention to the need of destroying the bridge over the Susquehanna River at Harrisburg and of disabling the Pennsylvania Railroad in order to sever communication with the west. "After that," he added, "I can turn my attention to Philadelphia, Baltimore, or Washington as may seem best for our interest."

Lee had suffered an irreparable loss at Chancellorsville when "Stonewall" Jackson was mortally wounded. Now reorganized into three infantry corps under Longstreet, A. P. Hill, and R. S. Ewell, and a cavalry division under J. E. B. Stuart, a changed Army of Northern Virginia faced the great test that lay ahead. "Stonewall" Jackson, the right hand of Lee, and in the words of the latter "the finest executive officer the sun ever shone on," was no longer present to lead his corps in battle.

The long lines of gray started moving on June 3 from Fredericksburg, Va., first northwestward across the Blue Ridge, then northward in the Shenandoah Valley. On June 9, one of the greatest cavalry engagements of the war occurred at Brandy Station. Union horsemen, for the first time, held Stuart's men on even terms. The Confederates then continued their march northward, with the right flank constantly protected by Stuart's cavalry, which occupied the passes of the Blue Ridge. Stuart was ordered to hold these mountain gaps until the advance into Pennsylvania had drawn the Union Army north of the Potomac. On June 28, Hill and Longstreet reached Chambersburg, 16 miles north of the Pennsylvania boundary. Rodes' division of Ewell's corps reached Carlisle on June 27. Early's command of 8,000 men had passed through Gettysburg on June 26 and on the 28th had reached York. Early planned to take possession of the bridge over the Susquehanna at Columbia, and to move on Harrisburg from the east. Lee's converging movement on Harrisburg seemed to be on the eve of success.

An unforeseen shift of events between June 25 and 28, however, threatened to deprive Lee of every advantage he had thus far gained in his daring march up the Shenandoah and Cumberland Valleys. The cavalry engagement between Stuart and Pleasonton at Brandy Station convinced Gen. Joseph Hooker, then in command of the Union Army, that the Confederate Army was moving northward. President Lincoln and General in Chief Halleck, informed of this movement, ordered

Hooker to proceed northward and to keep his command between the Confederate Army and Washington. When he was refused permission to abandon Harpers Ferry, and to add the garrison of 10,000 men to his army, Hooker asked to be relieved of command. Gen. George G. Meade received orders to assume command of the army at Frederick, Md., on June 28, and he at once continued the march northward.

General Stuart, in command of the Confederate cavalry, had obtained conditional approval from Lee to operate against the rear of the Union Army as it marched northward and then to join Lee north of the Potomac. As he passed between Hooker's army and Washington, the unexpected speed of the Union Army forced Stuart into detours and delays, so that on June 28 he was in eastern Maryland, wholly out of touch with the Confederate force. The eyes and ears of Lee were thus closed at a time when their efficient functioning was badly needed.

"Old Dorm" of Pennsylvania (now Gettysburg) **College.
It was used as a shelter for wounded.**

474-574 O-58—2

In this state of affairs, a Confederate agent reported to Lee at Chambersburg, Pa., on the night of June 28, that the Union forces had crossed the Potomac and were in the vicinity of Frederick. With the entire Union Army close at hand and with many miles between him and his base, Lee decided to abandon his original plan and to concentrate for battle. He moved his army at once across the mountains to Cashtown, 8 miles from Gettysburg. Here, in Cashtown Pass, he planned to establish his battle position. Rodes, then at Carlisle, and Early, at York, were at once ordered to this point.

The First Day

THE TWO ARMIES CONVERGE ON GETTYSBURG

The men of Heth's division, leading the Confederate advance across the mountain, reached Cashtown on June 29. Pettigrew's brigade was sent on to Gettysburg the following day to obtain supplies, but upon reaching the ridge a mile west of the town, they observed Union cavalry scouts posted along the roads. Not having orders to bring on an engagement, Pettigrew withdrew to Cashtown.

Scene of the initial engagement on the morning of July 1. 1. McPherson Ridge. 2. Oak Ridge.

In the intervening 2 days since he had assumed command of the Union forces, General Meade had moved his troops northward and instructed his engineers to survey a defensive battle position at Pipe Creek, near Taneytown, in northern Maryland. Buford's cavalry, which had effectively shadowed Lee's advance from the mountaintops of the Blue Ridge was ordered to make a reconnaissance in the Gettysburg area. It was these troops that Pettigrew's men saw posted on the roads leading into the town. Neither Lee nor Meade yet foresaw Gettysburg as a field of battle. Each expected to take a strong defensive position and force his adversary to attack.

Maj. Gen. John F. Reynolds.
(Courtesy National Archives.)

Lt. Gen. Ambrose P. Hill.
(Courtesy National Archives.)

A. P. Hill, in the absence of Lee, who was still beyond the mountains, now took the initiative. At daybreak of July 1, he ordered the brigades of Archer and Davis, of Heth's division, to advance along the Chambersburg Road to Gettysburg for the purpose of testing the strength of the Union forces. As these troops reached Marsh Creek, 4 miles from Gettysburg, they were fired upon by Union cavalry pickets who hurriedly retired to inform their commander of the enemy's approach. In the meantime, Buford's division of cavalry had moved from their camp just southwest of Gettysburg to McPherson Ridge, a mile west of the town. Buford prepared to hold out against heavy odds until aid arrived. Thus, subordinate field commanders had chosen the ground for battle.

It was 8 a. m., July 1, when the two brigades of Archer and Davis, the former to the right and the latter to the left of the Chambersburg Road, deployed on Herr Ridge. Supported by Pegram's artillery, they charged down the long slope and across Willoughby Run against Buford's men. The Union troopers had recently received an issue of Spencer repeating carbines. Dismounted, and fighting as infantrymen, they held their ground against the spirited attacks of Heth's superior numbers. At 10 o'clock timely aid arrived as troops from Gen. John F. Reynolds' First Infantry corps began streaming over Seminary Ridge from the south and relieved Buford's exhausted fighters. Calef's battery, one of whose guns had fired the first shot at Gettysburg, was replaced by Hall's Maine artillery. But, in a few moments, Union joy at receiving aid was offset by tragedy. Reynolds, close to the front lines, was killed instantly by a sharpshooter's bullet.

The struggle increased in scope as more forces reached the field. When Archer's Confederates renewed the attack across Willoughby Run, Union troops of Meredith's Iron Brigade, arriving opportunely, struck the flank of the Confederates and captured the greater part of the force, including General Archer. Relieved from the threat south of the Chambersburg Pike, the 14th Brooklyn and 7th Wisconsin regiments shifted to the north of the Pike where the Confederates had captured a part of Cutler's troops in the railroad cut. With renewed effort, these troops, joined by Dawes' 6th Wisconsin, drove the Confederates steadily back, capturing two Mississippi regiments in the defile. The Confederates then withdrew beyond striking distance. There was a lull in the fighting during the noon hour. The first encounter had given Union men confidence. They had held their ground against superior numbers and had captured Archer, a brigadier general, the first Confederate general officer taken since Lee assumed command.

McPherson Ridge and Woods, the Federal position on July 1. In the woods at the right, General Reynolds was killed. The cupola of the Theological Seminary appears in the background. (Brady photograph.)

THE BATTLE OF OAK RIDGE

While the initial test of strength was being determined west of Gettysburg by advance units, the main bulk of the two armies was pounding over the roads from the north and south, converging upon the ground chosen by Buford. Rodes' Confederates, hurrying southward from Carlisle to meet Lee at Cashtown, received orders at Biglerville to march to Gettysburg. Early, returning from York with Cashtown as his objective, learned at Heidlersburg of the action at Gettysburg and was ordered to approach by way of the Harrisburg Road.

Chambersburg Pike, looking westward from the Federal position toward Herr Ridge, where the Confederate attack began.

Employing the wooded ridge as a screen from Union cavalry north of Gettysburg, Rodes brought his guns into position on Oak Ridge about 1 o'clock and opened fire on the flank of Gen. Abner Doubleday, Reynolds' successor, on McPherson Ridge. The Union commander shifted his lines northeastward to Oak Ridge and the Mummasburg Road to meet the new attack. Rodes' Confederates struck the Union positions at the stone wall on the ridge, but the attack was not well coordinated and resulted in failure. Iverson's brigade was nearly annihilated as it made a left wheel to strike from the west. In the meantime, more Union troops had arrived on the field by way of the Taneytown Road. Two divisions of Howard's Eleventh corps were now taking position in the plain north of the town, intending to make contact with Doubleday's troops on Oak Ridge.

Doles' Confederate brigade charged across the plain and was able to force Howard's troops back temporarily, but it was the opportune approach of Early's division from the northeast on the Harrisburg Road which rendered the Union position north of Gettysburg indefensible. Arriving in the early afternoon as the Union men were establishing their position, Early struck with tremendous force, first with his artillery and then with his infantry, against General Barlow. Soon he had shattered the entire Union force. The remnants broke and turned southward through Gettysburg in the direction of Cemetery Hill. In this headlong and disorganized flight General Schimmelfenning was lost from his command, and, finding refuge in a shed, he lay 2 days concealed within the Confederate lines. In the path of Early's onslaught lay the youthful Brigadier Barlow severely wounded, and the gallant Lieut. Bayard Wilkeson, whose battery had long stood against overwhelming odds, mortally wounded.

Lt. Gen. Richard S. Ewell.
Courtesy National Archives.

Maj. Gen. Winfield S. Hancock.
Courtesy National Archives.

The Union men on Oak Ridge, faced with the danger that Doles would cut off their line of retreat, gave way and retired through Gettysburg to Cemetery Hill. The withdrawal of the Union troops from the north and northwest left the Union position on McPherson Ridge untenable. Early in the afternoon, when Rodes opened fire from Oak Hill, Heth had renewed his thrust along the Chambersburg Pike. His troops were soon relieved and Pender's division, striking north and south of the road, broke the Union line. The Union troops first withdrew to Seminary Ridge, then across the fields to Cemetery Hill. Here was advantageous ground which had been selected as a rallying point if the men were forced to relinquish the ground west and north of the town. Thus, by 5 o'clock, the remnants of the Union forces (some 6,000 out of the 18,000 engaged in the first day's struggle) were on the hills south of Gettysburg.

Ewell was now in possession of the town, and he extended his line from the streets eastward to Rock Creek. Studiously observing the hills in his front, he came within range of a Union sharpshooter, for suddenly he heard the thud of a minie ball. Calmly riding on, he remarked to General Gordon at his side, "You see how much better fixed for a fight I am than you are. It don't hurt at all to be shot in a wooden leg."

A momentous decision now had to be made. Lee had reached the field at 3 p. m., and had witnessed the retreat of the disorganized Union troops through the streets of Gettysburg. Through his glasses he had watched their attempt to reestablish their lines on Cemetery Hill. Sensing his advantage and a great opportunity, he sent orders to Ewell by a staff officer to "press those people" and secure the hill (Cemetery Hill) if possible. However, two of Ewell's divisions, those of Rodes and Early, had been heavily engaged throughout the afternoon and were not well in hand. Johnson's division could not reach the field until late in the evening, and the reconnaissance service of Stuart's cavalry was not yet available. General Ewell, uninformed of the Union strength in the rear of the hills south of Gettysburg, decided to await the arrival of Johnson's division. Cemetery Hill was not attacked, and Johnson, coming up late in the evening, stopped at the base of Culp's Hill. Thus passed Lee's opportunity of July 1.

Scene north of Gettysburg from Oak Ridge. The Federal position may be seen near the edge of the open fields in the middle distance.

When the Union troops retreated from the battleground north and west of the town on the evening of July 1, they hastily occupied defense positions on Cemetery Hill, Culp's Hill, and a part of Cemetery Ridge. Upon the arrival of Slocum by the Baltimore Pike and Sickles by way of the Emmitsburg Road, the Union right flank at Culp's Hill and Spangler's Spring and the important position at Little Round Top on the left were consolidated. Thus was developed a strong defensive battle line in the shape of a fish hook, about 3 miles long, with the advantage of high ground and of interior lines. Opposite, in a semicircle about 6 miles long, extending down Seminary Ridge and into the streets of Gettysburg, stood the Confederates who, during the night, had closed in from the north and west.

The greater part of the citizenry of Gettysburg, despite the prospect of battle in their own yards, chose to remain in their homes. Both army commanders respected noncombatant rights to a marked degree. Thus, in contrast with the fields of carnage all about the village, life and property of the civilian population remained unharmed, while the doors of churches, schools, and homes were opened for the care of the wounded.

General Meade, at Taneytown, had learned early in the afternoon of July 1 that a battle was developing and that Reynolds had been killed. A large part of his army was within 5 miles of Gettysburg. Meade then sent

General Hancock to study and report on the situation. Hancock reached the field just as the Union troops were falling back to Cemetery Hill. He helped to rally the troops and left at 6 o'clock to report to Meade that in his opinion the battle should be fought at Gettysburg. Meade acted on this recommendation and immediately ordered the concentration of the Union forces at that place. Meade himself arrived near midnight on July 1.

Spangler's Spring, the right of the Federal battle line of July 2 and 3. This view, made in 1870, shows the wartime appearance of the spring. (Tipton photograph.)

View of Culp's Hill, taken about 1890, showing earthworks on the crest of the hill. Gettysburg, one-half mile northwest, may be seen through the vista. (Tipton photograph.)

The Second Day

PRELIMINARY MOVEMENTS AND PLANS

The small college town of Gettysburg, with 2,400 residents at the time of the battle, lay in the heart of a fertile country, surrounded by broad acres of crops and pastures. Substantial houses of industrious Pennsylvania farmers dotted the countryside. South of the town and hardly more than a musket shot from the houses on its outer edge, Cemetery Hill rose somewhat abruptly from the lower ground. Extending southward from the hill for nearly 2 miles was a long roll of land called Cemetery Ridge. At its southern extremity a sharp incline terminated in the wooded crest of Little Round Top and a half mile beyond was the sugar-loaf peak of Big Round Top, the highest point in the vicinity of Gettysburg. Paralleling Cemetery Ridge, at an average distance of two-thirds of a mile to the west, lay Seminary Ridge, which derived its name from the Lutheran Seminary that stood upon its crest a half mile west of Gettysburg. In 1863, 10 roads radiated from Gettysburg, the one leading to Emmitsburg extending diagonally across the valley between Seminary and Cemetery Ridges.

Lunettes, or artillery defense works, on the crest of East Cemetery Hill. The entrance gateway to the public cemetery, which is still in use, appears in the background on the Baltimore Pike. (Brady photograph.)

Jennie Wade House, located on Baltimore street between the battle lines. Jennie Wade, the only civilian killed during the battle, was accidentally struck by a bullet which passed through a door of the house.

East Cemetery Hill, the objective of the Confederate charge on the evening of July 2.

By noon of July 2, the powerful forces of Meade and Lee were at hand, and battle on a tremendous scale was imminent. That part of the Union line extending from Cemetery Hill to Little Round Top was strongly held. Late in the forenoon, Sickles, commanding the Third Corps which lay north of Little Round Top, sent Berdan's sharpshooters and some of the men of the 3rd Maine Regiment forward from the Emmitsburg Road to Pitzer's Woods, a half mile to the west. As they reached the woods, a strong Confederate force fired upon them, and they hurriedly retired to inform their commander. To Sickles, the extension of the Confederate line southward meant that his left flank was endangered. He at once began moving forward to the advantageous high ground at the Peach Orchard, and by 3:30 p. m. his battle front extended from Devil's Den northwestward to the Orchard and northward on the Emmitsburg Road. In this forward movement, the strong position on the crest of Little Round Top was left unoccupied. This was the situation when Meade finally turned his attention from his right flank at Culp's Hill and Spangler's Spring—the cause of his great concern throughout the forenoon—to review Sickles' line.

Maj. Gen. Gouverneur K. Warren.
Courtesy National Archives.

Maj. Gen. Daniel E. Sickles.
Courtesy National Archives.

Lee planned to attack, despite the advice of Longstreet who continually urged defensive battle. On July 2, Longstreet recommended that Lee swing around the Union left at Little Round Top, select a good position, and await attack. Lee observed that while the Union position was strong if held in sufficient numbers to utilize the advantage of interior lines, it presented grave difficulties to a weak defending force. A secure lodgment on the shank of the hook might render it possible to sever the Union Army and to deal with each unit separately. Not all of Meade's force had reached the field, and Lee thought he had the opportunity of destroying his adversary in the process of concentration. He resolved to send Longstreet against the Federal left flank which he believed was then on lower Cemetery Ridge, while Ewell was to storm Cemetery Hill and Culp's Hill.

Trostle farmhouse. Here the 9th Massachusetts battery, taking position in the yard, lost 80 out of 88 horses during the battle of July 2. (Brady photograph.)

LONGSTREET ATTACKS ON THE RIGHT

In the execution of this plan, Longstreet was ordered to take position across the Emmitsburg Road and to attack what was thought to be the left flank of the Union line on Cemetery Ridge. From his encampment on the Chambersburg Road, 3 miles west of Gettysburg, he started toward his objective, using Herr Ridge to conceal the movement from Union signalmen on Little Round Top. After marching to Black Horse Tavern on the Fairfield Road, he realized that his troops were in sight of the signal unit and at once began retracing his course. Employing the trees on Seminary Ridge as a screen, he marched southward again in Willoughby Run Valley, arriving in position on the Emmitsburg Road about 3:30 p. m. Immediately in front, and only 700 yards away, Longstreet saw Sickles' batteries lined up in the Peach Orchard and on the Emmitsburg Road. Col. E. P. Alexander, commanding a battalion of Longstreet's artillery, opened with full force against the Union guns. Longstreet could observe in the distance that Little Round Top was unoccupied. Law's Alabama troops were directed at once to take the hill, and Robertson's Texans were instructed to join in the charge.

WARREN SAVES LITTLE ROUND TOP

Gen. G. K. Warren, Meade's Chief of Engineers, having assisted Sickles in placing his line, now rode to the crest of Little Round Top and found the hill, "the key to the Union position," unoccupied except by a signal station. Warren was informed by the signalmen that they believed Confederate troops lay concealed on the wooded ridge a mile to the west. Smith's New York battery, emplaced at Devil's Den, immediately was ordered to fire a shot into these woods. The missile, crashing through the trees, caused a sudden stir of the Confederates "which by the gleam of the reflected sunlight on their bayonets, revealed their long lines outflanking the position." Warren realized Longstreet would strike first at Little Round Top and he observed, too, the difficulty of shifting Sickles' position from Devil's Den to the hill.

The Wheatfield as it appeared in 1890. Little Round Top is in the background. (Tipton photograph.)

At this moment Warren noticed the approach of Union troops from the north and rode to meet them. They were Vincent's and Weed's brigades, leading Sykes' corps from reserve position to the front. Intercepting these troops, Warren rushed them to Little Round Top. Law's Alabama troops were starting to scale the south slope of the hill when Vincent's men rushed to the attack. Weed's brigade, following closely, drove over the crest and engaged Robertson's Texans on the west slope. The arrival of Hazlett's battery on the summit of the hill is thus described by an eyewitness: "The passage of the six guns through the roadless woods and amongst the rocks was marvelous. Under ordinary circumstances it would have been considered an impossible feat, but the eagerness of the men ... brought them without delay to the very summit, where they went immediately into battle." A desperate hand-to-hand struggle ensued. Weed and Hazlett were killed, and Vincent was mortally wounded—all young soldiers of great promise.

The struggle at Little Round Top now became stalemated, and Longstreet directed his entire line to attack. The Confederate drive was taken up in turn by the brigades of Benning, Anderson, Kershaw, Semmes, Barksdale, Wofford, Wilcox, Perry, and Wright against the divisions of Birney and Humphreys in the Wheatfield, the Peach Orchard, and along the Emmitsburg Road. Four hours of desperate fighting broke the Peach Orchard salient, an angle in the Union line which was struck from the south and the west. It left the Wheatfield strewn with dead and wounded, and the base of Little Round Top a shambles. Sickles' men had been driven back, and Longstreet was now in possession of the west slope of Big Round Top, of Devil's Den, and the Peach Orchard. Little Round Top, that commanding landmark from which Longstreet had hoped to shell the Union lines on Cemetery Ridge and Cemetery Hill, still remained in Union possession.

CULP'S HILL

In the Confederate plan, Ewell on the left was directed to attack Cemetery Hill and Culp's Hill in conjunction with Longstreet's drive. At the appointed time, the guns of Latimer's battalion on Benner's Hill, east of Gettysburg, opened a well-directed fire against the Union positions on East Cemetery Hill and Culp's Hill, but the return fire soon shattered many of Latimer's batteries and forced the remnants to retire out of range. In the final moments of this action the youthful Major Latimer was mortally wounded.

View of Little Round Top taken soon after the battle.
The crest and western slope of the hill had been cleared
the year preceding the battle. (Brady photograph.)

Breastworks constructed by Federal troops on Little
Round Top.

About dusk, long after the artillery fire had ceased, Early's infantry started a charge toward East Cemetery Hill. Seldom, if ever, surpassed in its dash and desperation, Early's assault reached the crest of the hill where the defenders, as a last resort in the hand-to-hand encounter, used clubbed muskets, stones, and rammers. Long after dark, the Louisiana Tigers and their comrades, in possession of the crest of the hill, fought to hold their gain and their captured guns. The failure of Rodes to move out of the streets of Gettysburg and to attack the hill from the west enabled Hancock to shift some of his men to aid in repelling Early's attacks. Faced by these Union reserves, Early's men finally gave way about 10 o'clock and sullenly retired to their lines. The Union troops stood firm.

Closely timed with Early's assault of East Cemetery Hill, Johnson's division charged the Union works on Culp's Hill. Failing to make headway, because of the steep incline and the strength of the Union positions, Johnson fell back across Rock Creek and started an attack on the southern slope of the hill. Here the Union works were thinly manned. An hour earlier, the divisions of Geary and Ruger had been called from those works to the aid of the Sickles line at the Peach Orchard. Johnson, finding the works weakly defended, took possession of them but did not press the attack farther. Only a few hundred yards away on the Baltimore Pike lay the Union supply trains. The failure of Confederate reconnaissance here again was critically important. Thus passed another opportunity to strike a hard blow at the Union Army.

The Third Day

CANNONADE AT DAWN: CULP'S HILL AND SPANGLER'S SPRING

Night brought an end to the bloody combat at East Cemetery Hill, but this was not the time for rest. What would Meade do? Would the Union Army remain in its established position and hold its lines at all costs? At midnight Meade sought the advice of his Council of War in the east room of his headquarters. The corps commanders—Gibbon, Williams, Sykes, Newton, Howard, Hancock, Sedgwick, and Slocum—without exception advised holding the positions established. Meade, approving, turned to the officer whose division held the Union center, and said, "Gibbon, if Lee attacks me tomorrow it will be on your front."

Meade on the following morning began to fortify Cemetery Ridge by shifting all units that could be spared from the line at Culp's Hill, and those in reserve at the Round Tops and on Cemetery Hill. General Hunt, Chief of Artillery, brought up reserve batteries to hold in readiness for replacement of front line guns. Throughout the forenoon of the third day, Meade not only developed a strong front at the stone walls on the crest of the ridge, but he also strengthened his reserve power to an extent which rendered the Union center almost impregnable.

Interior of breastworks on Little Round Top.
(Brady photograph.)

Meanwhile, important movements were occurring elsewhere on the field. Ruger's division and Lockwood's brigade, which had been called from their lines on the south slope of Culp's Hill the previous evening to help defend Sickles' position at the Peach Orchard, were now countermarching, under cover of darkness, to reoccupy their ground. Geary, who had misunderstood orders and had marched down the Baltimore Pike, was also returning to his works. Ruger's men, upon reaching the Pike, learned from scouts that their entrenchments south of Culp's Hill and at Spangler's Spring had been occupied by the Confederates. Ruger, resolving upon an attack at daybreak, organized his forces along the Pike. Powerful artillery units under Muhlenberg were brought into place along the road; Rigby's Maryland battery was stationed on Power's Hill, a prominent knoll a half mile to the south; and another battery was emplaced on McAllister Hill.

Lt. Gen. James Longstreet.
Courtesy National Archives.

Col. Edward Porter Alexander.
Courtesy National Archives.

As dawn broke on July 3, Union guns on the Baltimore Pike opened with a heavy cannonade on Johnson's Confederates at Spangler's Spring. The heavily wooded area about the Confederate lines prevented them from bringing guns into position to return the fire. Union skirmishers began streaming across the field toward the Confederate entrenchments. The full force of Ruger's and Geary's brigades followed closely. Throughout the forenoon the Union troops struck again and again.

It was about 10 o'clock that Ruger, believing that a flank attack might break the resistance of Johnson's men, ordered Col. Silas Colgrove to strike the Confederate left flank near the spring. The troops of the 2d Massachusetts and the 19th Indiana regiments started across the swale from the cover of the woods on the little hill south of the spring. A withering fire slowed their pace, but they charged on, only to have their ranks decimated by the Confederates in strong positions back of a stone wall. Colonel Mudge, inspiring leader of the Massachusetts regiment, fell mortally wounded. Forced to fall back, the men soon learned their efforts had not been in vain. On Ruger's and Geary's front the Confederates were now giving way and soon had retired across Rock Creek, out of striking range. By 11 o'clock, the Union troops were again in possession of their earthworks; again they could quench their thirst in the cooling waters of the spring.

LEE PLANS A FINAL THRUST

General Lee must have learned by mid-forenoon, after the long hours of struggle at Culp's Hill and Spangler's Spring, that his troops could not hold the Union works which they had occupied with so little effort the previous evening. He had seen, also, that in the tremendous battling during the preceding afternoon no important gains had been made at Little Round Top and its vicinity. Longstreet had gained the advantageous ridge at the Peach Orchard and had brought his batteries forward from Pitzer's Woods to this high ground in preparation for a follow-up attack. Wright's brigade, the last unit to move forward on July 2 in the echelon attack begun by General Law, had charged across the open fields at dusk and pierced the Union center just south of the copse of trees on Cemetery Ridge. Wright's success could not be pressed to decisive advantage as the brigades on his left had not moved forward to his support, and he was forced to retire. Again, lack of coordination in attack was to count heavily against the Confederates.

The failure to make any pronounced headway on July 2 at Culp's Hill and Little Round Top, and the momentary success of Wright on Cemetery Ridge, doubtless led Lee to believe that Meade's flanks were strong and his center weak. A powerful drive at the center might pierce the enemy's lines and fold them back. The shattered units might then be destroyed or captured at will. Such a charge across open fields and in the face of frontal and flank fire would, Lee well understood, be a gamble seldom undertaken. Longstreet strongly voiced his objection to such a move, insisting that "no 15,000 men ever arrayed for battle can take that position."

**View of the Peach Orchard and the Emmitsburg Road in 1890.
The Wentz farm buildings appear at the left.**
(Tipton photograph.)

**Devil's Den, a formation of large granite boulders,
used as defense positions by Confederate sharpshooters.**

Time now was the important element. Whatever could be done must be done quickly. Hood's and McLaws' divisions, who had fought bravely and lost heavily at Round Top and the Wheatfield, were not in condition for another severe test. Early and Johnson on the left had likewise endured long, unrelenting battle with powerful Union forces in positions of advantage. The men of Heth's and Pender's divisions had not been heavily engaged since the first day's encounter west of Gettysburg. These were the men, along with Pickett's division, whom Lee would have to count on to bear the brunt of his final great effort at Gettysburg.

LEE AND MEADE SET THE STAGE

Late in the forenoon of July 3, General Meade had completed his plan of defense in rear of the Union center by the concentration of all available infantry units. General Hunt, sensing the danger, placed a solid line of batteries in position on the crest of the ridge and brought others to the rear for emergency use. As a final act of preparation, Meade inspected his front at the stone wall, then rode southward to Little Round Top. Here, with General Warren, he could see the long lines of Confederate batteries and the massing of troops, a sure indication of attack. Meade rode back to his headquarters.

Lee, on his part, had observed in the forenoon the enemy in the process of concentration on Cemetery Ridge. Having reached his decision to strike the Union center, he had already begun the movement of batteries from the rear to points of advantage. By noon, 138 guns were in line from the Peach Orchard northward to the Seminary buildings, many of them only 800 yards from the Union center. To Colonel Alexander fell the lot of directing the artillery fire and informing the infantry of the best opportunity to advance.

Massed to the west of Emmitsburg Road, on low ground which screened their position from the Union lines, lay Gen. George Pickett's three brigades commanded by Kemper, Armistead, and Garnett. Pickett's men had arrived the previous evening from Chambersburg, where they had guarded Lee's wagons on July 1 and 2. As the only fresh body of troops on the field, they were now to spearhead the charge. On Pickett's left, the attacking front was fast being organized. Joseph Pettigrew, a brigadier, was preparing to lead the division of the wounded Major General Heth and Maj. Gen. Isaac Trimble took the command of Pender. More than 10,000 troops of these two divisions—including such units as the 26th North Carolina whose losses on the first day were so heavy that the dead marked their advance "with the accuracy of a line at a dress parade"—now awaited the order to attack. Many hours earlier, the Bliss farm buildings, which lay in their front, had been burned. Their objective on the ridge was in clear view. The brigades of Wilcox and Lang were to move forward on the right of Pickett in order to protect his flank as he neared the enemy position.

**The Round Tops as they appear from Longstreet's
battle line one mile away.**

General Stuart, in the meantime, had been out of touch with Lee. Moving northward on the right flank of the Union Army, he became involved in a sharp engagement at Hanover, Pa., on June 30. Seeking to regain contact with Lee, he arrived at Carlisle on the evening of July 1. As he began shelling the barracks, orders arrived from Lee and he at once marched for Gettysburg, arriving north of the town the next day. Lee now decided to employ his cavalry to cut off Union retreat which might result from a successful attack on the center. Stuart was instructed to swing eastward and then south around Gettysburg the morning of July 3 in order to arrive in the rear of the Union lines at the time Pickett was expected to charge the center.

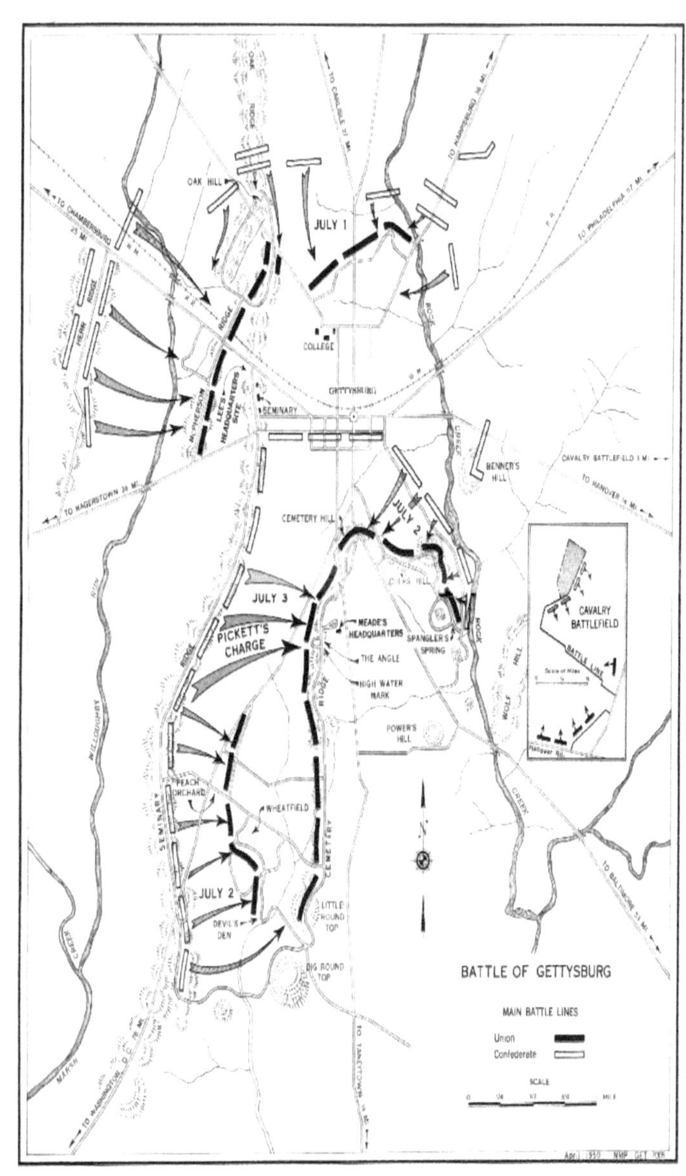

BATTLE OF GETTYSBURG

View northward from Little Round Top. 1. Cemetery Ridge. 2. Cemetery Hill. 3. Field of Pickett's Charge. 4. Seminary Ridge. 5. Oak Hill. The statue of G. K. Warren appears in the foreground.

Meade's headquarters as it appears today.

Except for the intermittent sniping of sharpshooters, an ominous silence prevailed over the fields. The orders had now been given; the objective had been pointed out. Men talked of casual things. Some munched on hard bread, others looked fearfully to the eastward, where, with the same mixed feelings, lay their adversary.

Far to the south, on another crucial front, General Pemberton was penning a letter to General Grant asking terms for the surrender of Vicksburg. In Richmond, the sick and anxious Jefferson Davis looked hopefully for heartening word from his great field commander at Gettysburg. The outcome of this bold venture would count heavily in the balance for the cause of the Confederacy.

ARTILLERY DUEL AT ONE O'CLOCK

At 1 o'clock two guns of Miller's Battery, posted near the Peach Orchard, opened fire in rapid succession. It was the signal for the entire line to let loose their terrific blast. Gunners rushed to their cannon, and in a few moments the massed batteries shook the countryside. Firing in salvos and in succession, the air was soon filled with smoke and heavy dust, which darkened the sky. Union gunners on Cemetery Ridge waited a few minutes until the positions of the Confederate batteries were located; then 80 guns, placed it close order, opened fire. For nearly 2 hours the duel continued, then that Union fire slackened. Hunt had ordered a partial cessation in order to cool the guns and to replace broken carriages.

Panorama of the battlefield from Cemetery Ridge. 1. General Meade statue. 2. Cemetery Ridge (Union position). **3. Little Round Top. 4. Big Round Top. 5. Devil's Den. 6. High Water Mark—farthest advance of Pickett's Charge. 7. The Wheatfield. 8. The Angle. 9. The Peach Orchard. 10. Codori Buildings. 11. Field of Pickett's Charge. 12. Emmitsburg Road. 13. Seminary Ridge** (Confederate position). **14. Virginia Memorial.**

Colonel Alexander, in position on the Emmitsburg Road near the Peach Orchard, could observe the effectiveness of his fire on the Union lines and also keep the Confederate troops in view. To him, it appeared that Union artillery fire was weakening. His own supply of ammunition was running low. Believing this was the time to attack, Alexander sent a message to Pickett who in turn rode over to Longstreet. General Longstreet, who had persistently opposed Lee's plan of sending 15,000 men across the open ground, was now faced with a final decision. Longstreet merely nodded approval and Pickett saluted, saying, "I am going to move forward, sir." He rode back to his men and ordered the advance. With Kemper on the right, Garnett on the left, and Armistead a few yards to the rear, the division marched out in brigade front, first northeastward into the open fields, then eastward toward the Union lines. As Pickett's men came into view near the woods, Pettigrew and Trimble gave the order to advance. The troops of the Carolinas, Tennessee, and Mississippi, comprising the brigades of Mayo, Davis, Marshall, and Fry in front, followed closely by Lane and Lowrance, now moved out to attack. A gap of half a mile between Pickett's left and Pettigrew's right would be closed as the advance progressed. The units were to converge as they approached the Union lines so that the final stage of the charge would present a solid front.

CLIMAX AT GETTYSBURG

Billows of smoke lay ahead of the Union men at the stone wall, momentarily obscuring the enemy. But trained observers on Little Round Top, far to the south, could see in the rear of this curtain of smoke the waves of Confederates starting forward. Pickett, finding his brigades drifting southeastward, ordered them to bear to the left, and the men turned toward the copse of trees. Kemper was now approaching on the south of the Codori buildings; Garnett and Armistead were on the north. Halted momentarily at the Emmitsburg Road to remove fence rails, Pickett's troops, with Pettigrew on the left, renewed the advance. Pickett had anticipated frontal fire of artillery and infantry from the strong Union positions at the stone walls on the ridge, but now an unforeseen attack developed. Union guns as far south as Little Round Top, along with batteries on Cemetery Hill, relieved from Confederate fire at the Seminary buildings, opened on the right and left flanks. As Pickett's men drove toward the Union works at The Angle, Stannard's Vermont troops, executing a right turn movement from their position south of the copse, fired into the flank of the charging Confederates.

The advancing lines crumbled, re-formed, and again pressed ahead under terrific fire from the Union batteries.

Maj. Gen. J. E. B. Stuart.
Courtesy National Archives.

Maj. Gen. George E. Pickett.
Courtesy National Archives.

A hundred yards from the stone wall, in the tall grass, they encountered Union skirmishers who fired and hastily withdrew. But all along the wall the Union infantry opened with volley after volley into the depleted ranks of Garnett and Fry. Armistead closed in, and with Lane and Lowrance joining him, made a last concerted drive. At this close range, double canister and concentrated infantry fire cut wide gaps in the attacking front. Garnett was mortally wounded; Kemper was down, his lines falling away on the right and left. Armistead reached the low stone fence. In a final surge, he crossed the wall with 150 men and, with his cap on his sword, shouted "Follow me!" At the peak of the charge, he fell mortally wounded. From the ridge, Union troops rushed forward and Hall's Michigan regiments let loose a blast of musketry. The gray column was surrounded. The tide of the Confederacy had "swept to its crest, paused, and receded."

Two of the divisions in the charge were reduced to mere fragments. In front of the Union line, 20 fallen battle flags lay in a space of 100 yards square. Singly and in little clumps, the remnants of the gray columns that had made the magnificent charge of a few minutes earlier now sullenly retreated across the fields toward the Confederate lines. Lee, who had watched anxiously from Spangler's Woods, now rode out to meet his men. "All this has been my fault," he said to General Wilcox who had brought off his command after heavy losses. "It is I that have lost this fight, and you must help me out of it in the best way you can." And again that night, in a moment of contemplation, he remarked to a comrade, "Too bad! too bad! Oh! too bad!"

The Angle, showing the stone wall and the fields' over which Pickett's troops charged. The Virginia Memorial appears in the background on Seminary Ridge.

The High Water Mark Monument, which marks the farthest
advance made by the Confederates against the Federal
position in Pickett's Charge.

CAVALRY ACTION

As the strength of Lee's mighty effort at The Angle was ebbing and the
scattered remnants of the charge were seeking shelter, action of a
different kind was taking place on another field not far distant. Early in
the afternoon, Stuart's cavalry was making its way down the valley of
Cress Run, 3 miles east of Gettysburg. The brigades of Hampton and
Fitzhugh Lee, at the rear of the line of march, momentarily lost the trail
and came out into open ground at the north end of Rummel's Woods.
Stuart, soon learning of the mistake, attempted to bring them into line
and to proceed southward. But at this point, Gen. D. M. Gregg's Union
cavalry, in position along the Hanover Road a mile southeast, saw the
Confederates. Gregg prepared at once to attack, and Stuart had no
choice but to fight on this ground. As the two forces moved closer,
dismounted men opened a brisk fire, supported by the accurate shelling
of artillerists.

Section of the Cyclorama painting of Pickett's Charge by Paul Philippoteaux. Courtesy Times and News Publishing Company.

The General Hospital one mile east of Gettysburg. A few weeks after the battle the Union and Confederate wounded were removed to this place from field hospitals in the rear of the battle lines.
(Brady photograph.)

Then came the initial cavalry charge and countercharge. The Confederate Jenkins was forced to withdraw when his small supply of ammunition became exhausted. Hampton, Fitzhugh Lee, and Chambliss charged again and again, only to be met with the equally spirited counterattack of McIntosh. Custer's Michigan regiments closed in on a flank movement against the right of the charging Confederate troopers, and Miller's squadron of the 3d Pennsylvania, disobeying orders to hold its position, struck opportunely on the Confederate left. The thrusts of the Union horsemen, so well coordinated, stopped the onslaught of Stuart's troopers. After 3 hours of driving assaults, the Confederates left the field and retired to the north of Gettysburg. The Union horsemen, holding their ground, had successfully cut off the prospect of Confederate cavalry aid in the rear of the Union lines on Cemetery Ridge.

End of Invasion

Lee, as he looked over the desolate field of dead and wounded and the broken remnants of his once-powerful army still ready for renewed battle, must have realized that not only was Gettysburg lost, but that eventually it might all end this way. Meade did not counterattack, as expected. The following day, July 4, the two armies lay facing each other, exhausted and torn.

During the 75th anniversary of the Battle of Gettysburg, July 1-4, 1938, 1,845 soldiers attended the Federal and Confederate reunion. Here veterans of the two armies clasp hands across the stone wall at The Angle.

Late on the afternoon of July 4, Lee began an orderly retreat. The wagon train of wounded, 17 miles in length, guarded by Imboden's cavalry, started homeward through Greenwood and Greencastle. At night, the able-bodied men marched over the Hagerstown Road by way of Monterey Pass to the Potomac. Roads had become nearly impassable from the heavy rains that day. So well did Stuart cover the retreat that the army reached the Potomac with comparatively little loss. Meade, realizing that the Confederate Army was actually retreating and not retiring to the mountain passes, sent his cavalry and Sedgwick's corps of infantry in pursuit and ordered the mountain passes west of Frederick covered. Lee, having the advantage of the more direct route to the Potomac, reached the river several days ahead of his pursuers, but heavy rains had swollen the current and he could not cross. Meade arrived on the night of July 12 and prepared for a general attack. On the following night, however, the river receded and Lee crossed safely into Virginia. The Confederate Army, Meade's critics said, had been permitted to slip from the Union grasp.

The Eternal Light Peace Memorial, dedicated on the 75th anniversary of the battle, commemorates "Peace Eternal in a Nation United."

Lincoln and Gettysburg

ESTABLISHMENT OF A BURIAL GROUND

For the residents of Gettysburg the aftermath of battle was almost as trying as the 3 days of struggle that had swirled about them. The town's 2,400 inhabitants, and the nearby country folk, bore a heavy share of the burden of caring for the 21,000 wounded and dying of both sides, who were left behind when the armies moved on. Spacious rooms in churches and schools and hundreds of homes were turned over to the care of the wounded; and kindly folk from neighboring towns came to help those of Gettysburg in ministering to the needs of the maimed and shattered men.

Adequate attention to the wounded was an immediate necessity, but fully as urgent was the need of caring for the dead. Nearly 6,000 had been killed in action, and hundreds died each day from mortal wounds. In the earlier stages of the battle, soldiers of both armies performed the tasks of burying their fallen comrades, but the struggle had reached such large proportions and the scene of battle had so shifted that fallen men had come within enemy lines. Because of the emergencies of battle, therefore, hundreds of bodies had been left unburied or only partially covered. It was evident that the limited aid which could be offered by local authorities must be supported by a well-organized plan for disinterment of the dead from the temporary burial grounds on the field and reburial in a permanent place at Gettysburg or in home cemeteries.

A few days after the battle, the Governor of the Commonwealth, Hon. Andrew Curtin, visited the battlefield to offer assistance in caring for the wounded. When official duties required his return to Harrisburg, he appointed Attorney David Wills, of Gettysburg, to act as his special agent. At the time of his visit, the Governor was especially distressed by the condition of the dead. In response to the Governor's desire that the remains be brought together in a place set aside for the purpose, Mr. Wills selected land on the northern slope of Cemetery Hill and suggested that the State of Pennsylvania purchase the ground at once in order that interments could begin without delay. He proposed that contributions for the purpose of laying out and landscaping the grounds be asked from legislatures of the States whose soldiers had taken part in the battle.

Within 6 weeks, Mr. Wills had purchased 17 acres of ground on Cemetery Hill and engaged William Saunders, an eminent landscape gardener, to lay out the grounds in State lots, apportioned in size to the number of graves for the fallen of each State. Each of the Union States represented in the battle made contributions for planning and landscaping.

The reinterment of 3,512 bodies in the cemetery was accomplished only after many months. Great care had been taken to identify the bodies on the field, and, at the time of reinterment, remains were readily identified by marked boards which had been placed at the field grave or by items found on the bodies. Even so, the names of 1,664 remained unknown, 979 of whom were without identification either by name or by State. Within a year, appropriations from the States made possible the enclosure of the cemetery with a massive stone wall and an iron fence on the Baltimore Street front, imposing gateways of iron, headstones for the graves, and a keeper's lodge. Since the original burials, the total of Civil War interments has reached 3,706. Including those of later wars, the total number now is 4,399.

**Photograph of Lincoln taken a few days before
he left Washington en route to Gettysburg, November 1863.**
(Gardner photograph.)

The Soldiers' National Monument, commemorating the Federal dead who fell at Gettysburg, was dedicated July 1, 1869. It is located at the place where Lincoln delivered his Gettysburg Address.

The removal of Confederate dead from the field burial plots was not undertaken until 7 years after the battle. During the years 1870-73, upon the initiative of the Ladies Memorial Associations of Richmond, Raleigh, Savannah, and Charleston, 3,320 bodies were disinterred and sent to cemeteries in those cities for reburial, 2,935 being interred in Hollywood Cemetery, Richmond. Seventy-three bodies were reburied in home cemeteries.

The Commonwealth of Pennsylvania incorporated the cemetery in January 1864. The cemetery "having been completed, and the care of it by Commissioners from so many states being burdensome and expensive," the Board of Commissioners, authorized by act of the General Assembly of Pennsylvania in 1868, recommended the transfer of the cemetery to the Federal Government. The Secretary of War accepted title to the cemetery for the United States Government on May 1, 1872.

DEDICATION OF THE CEMETERY

Having agreed upon a plan for the cemetery, the Commissioners believed it advisable to consecrate the grounds with appropriate ceremonies. Mr. Wills, representing the Governor of Pennsylvania, was selected to make proper arrangements for the event. With the approval of the Governors of the several States, he wrote to Hon. Edward Everett, of Massachusetts, inviting him to deliver the oration on the occasion and suggested October 23, 1863, as the date for the ceremony. Mr. Everett stated in reply that the invitation was a great compliment, but that because of the time necessary for the preparation of the oration he could not accept a date earlier than November 19. This was the date agreed upon.

Edward Everett was the outstanding orator of his day. He had been a prominent Boston minister and later a university professor. A cultured scholar, he had delivered orations on many notable occasions. In a distinguished career he became successively President of Harvard, Governor of Massachusetts, United States Senator, Minister to England, and Secretary of State.

The Wills house where Lincoln was a guest when the national cemetery was dedicated.

The Gettysburg cemetery, at the time of the dedication, was not under the authority of the Federal Government. It had not occurred to those in charge, therefore, that the President of the United States might desire to attend the ceremony. When formally printed invitations were sent to a rather extended list of national figures, including the President, the acceptance from Mr. Lincoln came as a surprise. Mr. Wills was thereupon instructed to request the President to take part in the program, and, on November 2, a personal invitation was addressed to him.

**The procession on Baltimore Street en route to the
cemetery for the dedicatory exercises, November 19.**

Throngs filled the town on the evening of November 18. The special train from Washington bearing the President arrived in Gettysburg at dusk. Mr. Lincoln was escorted to the spacious home of Mr. Wills on Center Square. Sometime later in the evening the President was serenaded, and at a late hour he retired. At 10 o'clock on the following morning, the appointed time for the procession to begin, Mr. Lincoln was ready. The various units of the long procession, marshaled by Ward Lamon, began moving on Baltimore Street, the President riding horseback. The elaborate order of march also included Cabinet officials, judges of the Supreme Court, high military officers, Governors, commissioners, the Vice President, the Speaker of the House of Representatives, Members of Congress, and many local groups.

Difficulty in getting the procession under way and the tardy return of Mr. Everett from his drive over the battleground accounted for a delay of an hour in the proceedings. At high noon, with thousands scurrying about for points of vantage, the ceremonies were begun with the playing of a dirge by one of the bands. As the audience stood uncovered, a prayer was offered by Rev. Thomas H. Stockton, Chaplain of the House of Representatives. "Old Hundred" was played by the Marine Band. Then Mr. Everett arose, and "stood a moment in silence, regarding the battlefield and the distant beauty of the South Mountain range." For nearly 2 hours he reviewed the funeral customs of Athens, spoke of the purposes of war, presented a detailed account of the 3-days' battle, offered tribute to those who died on the battlefield, and reminded his audience of the bonds which are common to all Americans. Upon the conclusion of his address, a hymn was sung.

First page of the second draft of the Gettysburg Address. This copy, made by Lincoln on the morning of November 19, was held in his hand while delivering his address. Reproduced from the original in the Library of Congress.

**This photograph is the only known close-up view of the rostrum
(upper left) at the dedication of the national cemetery. The view shows
a part of the audience which was estimated at 15,000.**
(Bachrach photograph.)

Then the President arose and spoke his immortal words:

Four score and seven years ago our fathers brought forth on this continent, a new nation, conceived in Liberty, and dedicated to the proposition that all men are created equal.

Now we are engaged in a great civil war, testing whether that nation, or any nation so conceived and so dedicated, can long endure. We are met on a great battle field of that war. We have come to dedicate a portion of that field, as a final resting place for those who here gave their lives that that nation might live. It is altogether fitting and proper that we should do this.

But, in a larger sense, we cannot dedicate—we cannot consecrate—we cannot hallow—this ground. The brave men, living and dead, who struggled here, have consecrated it, far above our poor power to add or detract. The world will little note, nor long remember what we say here, but it can never forget what they did here. It is for us the living, rather, to be dedicated here to the unfinished work which they who fought here have thus far so nobly advanced. It is rather for us to be here dedicated to the great task remaining before us—that from these honored dead we take increased devotion to that cause for which they gave the last full measure of devotion—that we here highly resolve that these dead shall not have died in vain—that this nation, under God, shall have a new birth of freedom—and that government of the people, by the people, for the people, shall not perish from the earth.

A hymn was then sung and Rev. H. L. Baugher pronounced the benediction.

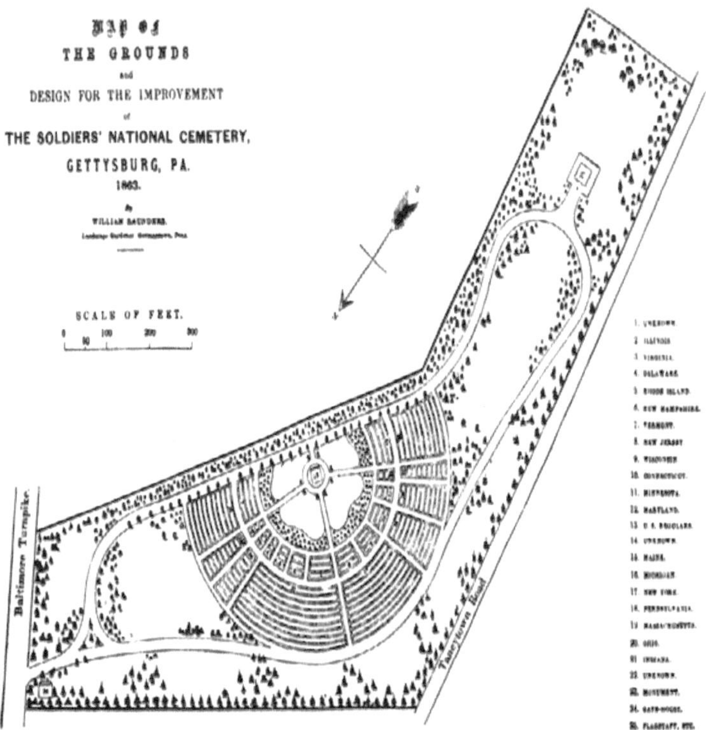

Plan of the national cemetery drawn in the autumn of 1863 by the notable landscape gardener, William Saunders.

MAP OF
THE GROUNDS
and
DESIGN FOR THE IMPROVEMENT
of
THE SOLDIERS' NATIONAL CEMETERY,
GETTYSBURG, PA.
1863.
By
WILLIAM SAUNDERS,
Landscape Gardener Germantown, Penn.

1. UNKNOWN.

2. ILLINOIS.

3. VIRGINIA.

4. DELAWARE.

5. RHODE ISLAND.

6. NEW HAMPSHIRE.

7. VERMONT.

8. NEW JERSEY.

9. WISCONSIN.

10. CONNECTICUT.

11. MINNESOTA.

12. MARYLAND.

13. U. S. REGULARS.

14. UNKNOWN.

15. MAINE.

16. MICHIGAN

17. NEW YORK.

18. PENNSYLVANIA.

19. MASSACHUSETTS.

20. OHIO.

21. INDIANA.

22. UNKNOWN.

23. MONUMENT.

24. GATE-HOUSE.

25. FLAGSTAFF, ETC.

The Lincoln Address Memorial, the only monument ever erected to commemorate an address, stands near the west gate of the national cemetery.

GENESIS OF THE GETTYSBURG ADDRESS

The theme of the Gettysburg Address was not entirely new. "Must a government, of necessity, be too strong for the liberties of its people," Lincoln had once asked, "or too weak to maintain its own existence?" Speaking of war aims, he said, "We shall nobly save, or meanly lose, the last best hope of earth." When he referred at Gettysburg to "the unfinished work which they who fought here have thus far so nobly advanced," he had in mind the high purpose of the preservation of the Union and the welfare of all the people. More than a year after Gettysburg, Lincoln in his Second Inaugural address uttered words which might very well be considered a companion sentiment to those expressed at Gettysburg: "With malice toward none; with charity for all; with firmness in the right as God gives us to see the right." This profession of faith came from the heart of a man of humility who sought then, as he did throughout the war, to assuage suffering and anxiety everywhere.

Rather than accept the address as a few brief notes hastily prepared on the route to Gettysburg (an assumption which has long gained much public acceptance), it should be regarded as a pronouncement of the high purpose dominant in Lincoln's thinking throughout the war. Habitually cautious of words in public address, spoken or written, it is not likely that the President, on such an occasion, failed to give careful thought to the words which he would speak. After receiving the belated invitation on November 2, he yet had ample time to prepare for the occasion, and the well-known correspondent Noah Brooks stated that several days before the dedication Lincoln told him in Washington that his address would be "short, short, short" and that it was "written, but not finished."

THE FIVE AUTOGRAPH COPIES OF THE GETTYSBURG ADDRESS

Even after his arrival at Gettysburg the President continued to put finishing touches to his address. The first page of the original text was written in ink on a sheet of Executive Mansion paper. The second page, either written or revised at the Wills residence, was in pencil on a sheet of foolscap, and, according to Lincoln's secretary, Nicolay, the few words changed in pencil at the bottom of the first page were added while in Gettysburg. The second draft of the address was written in Gettysburg probably on the morning of its delivery, as it contains certain phrases that are not in the first draft but are in the reports of the address as delivered and in subsequent copies made by Lincoln. It is probable, as stated in the explanatory note accompanying the original copies of the first and second drafts in the Library of Congress, that it was the second draft which Lincoln held in his hand when he delivered the address.

Quite opposite to Lincoln's feeling, expressed soon after the delivery of the address, that it "would not scour," the President lived long enough to think better of it himself and to see it widely accepted as a masterpiece. Early in 1864, Mr. Everett requested him to join in presenting manuscripts of the two addresses given at Gettysburg to be bound in a volume and sold for the benefit of stricken soldiers at a Sanitary Commission Fair in New York. The draft Lincoln sent became the third autograph copy, known as the Everett-Keyes copy, and it is now in the possession of the Illinois State Historical Library.

George Bancroft requested a copy in April 1864, to be included in *Autograph Leaves of Our Country's Authors*. This volume was to be sold at a Soldiers' and Sailors' Sanitary Fair in Baltimore. As this fourth copy was written on both sides of the paper, it proved unusable for this purpose, and Mr. Bancroft was allowed to keep it. This autograph draft is known as the Bancroft copy, as it remained in that family for many years. It has recently been presented to the Cornell University Library. Finding that the copy written for *Autograph Leaves* could not be used, Mr. Lincoln wrote another, a fifth draft, which was accepted for the purpose requested. It is the only draft to which he affixed his signature. In all probability it was the last copy written by Lincoln, and because of the apparent care in its preparation it has become the standard version of the address. The fifth draft, which long remained in the hands of the family of Col. Alexander Bliss, publisher of *Autograph Leaves*, is known as the Bliss copy. It was purchased in 1949 by Oscar B. Cintas, of Havana, Cuba.

SOLDIERS' NATIONAL MONUMENT

As a fitting memorial to the Union dead who fell at Gettysburg, the Commissioners arranged for the erection of a monument in the center of the semicircular plot of graves. A design submitted by J. G. Batterson was accepted and the services of Randolph Rogers, a distinguished American sculptor, were secured for the execution of the monument. Projecting from the four angles of the gray granite shaft are allegorical statues in white marble representing War, History, Peace, and Plenty. Surmounting the shaft is a white marble statue representing the Genius of Liberty. Known as the Soldiers' National Monument, the cornerstone was laid July 4, 1865, and the monument dedicated July 1, 1869.

THE LINCOLN ADDRESS MEMORIAL

The "few appropriate remarks" of Lincoln at Gettysburg came to be accepted with the passing of years not only as a fine expression of the purposes for which the war was fought, but as a masterpiece of literature. An effort to have the words of the martyr President commemorated on this battlefield culminated with the inclusion in the act approved February 12, 1895, which established Gettysburg National Military Park, of a provision for the erection of such a memorial. Pursuant to this authority, the Park Commission erected the Lincoln Address Memorial, in January 1912, near the west gate of the national cemetery.

The national cemetery

Guide Tour of the Park—(See map on page 75)

The self-guide tour of the park begins on McPherson Ridge, a mile west of Gettysburg. Upon arrival in Gettysburg, the visitor should first locate Center Square, then drive a mile westward on U. S. No. 30 to the statues of Generals Reynolds and Buford.

STOP 1. MCPHERSON RIDGE

(Please face westward, with the statue of Reynolds on your right.)

The Battle of Gettysburg began on this ridge at 8 a. m., July 1, 1863. The Confederate Army, approaching along the Chambersburg Pike, formed line of battle on the ridge one-half mile westward where you see the brick house (Herr Tavern). They first attacked the Union cavalry on this ridge, then infantry on the ridge 200 yards to your rear. In the afternoon, the Confederates renewed their drive from the west along the Pike and also struck the Union right flank (Oak Hill, No. 2 on Tour Map). The Union forces finally gave way, retreating first to the Seminary buildings and then to Cemetery Hill south of Gettysburg.

General Reynolds, commanding a Union corps, was killed in the woods a quarter of a mile southeast of this point. Buford, whose statue is just in front of you, commanded the Union cavalry on this ridge. The marked gun at the base of the Buford statue fired the first cannon shot at Gettysburg. Oak Ridge lies one-half mile back of you, and the same wooded ridge extending south of the Chambersburg Pike is Seminary Ridge.

General Lee, the Confederate commander, used the valley beyond the South Mountains (to the west) as an avenue of approach into Pennsylvania.

STOP 2. OAK HILL

(Please face southward with the Peace Memorial to your rear.)

The Battle of Gettysburg, which began at 8 a. m., on the two ridges a mile south of here, halted at noon, and the Confederates withdrew. At 1 o'clock, a strong Confederate force arrived from the north on this hill and fired into the flank of the Union men on the ridges to the south. Faced with this powerful fire and with renewed attack from the west, part of the Union forces were shifted to Oak Ridge (see monuments on the ridge to your left) to meet the attack from this direction. Union troops on the plain east of this ridge were soon forced by another strong Confederate charge to retreat headlong through the streets of Gettysburg, opening the Union line on Oak Ridge to flank and rear attack. By mid-afternoon, the Union position on Oak Ridge was abandoned, and the Confederates pursued the retreating Union troops through Gettysburg, halting in the western part of the town.

The gap in the South Mountains to your right is Cashtown Pass where Lee's army crossed the range.

STOP 3. OAK RIDGE

(Please face eastward toward the monuments on the plain.)

When Rodes' Confederate troops reached Oak Hill at 1 o'clock, Union troops on McPherson Ridge, as well as reserves, were shifted hurriedly to this ground. The Union troops, posted back of the stone wall, faced the Confederate charge from the west and north. Tenaciously holding this ground through repeated Confederate attacks, the Union men were finally forced to give way. Howard's Union corps had arrived earlier in the plain north of Gettysburg (see monuments to the east) but his command was soon shattered by a Confederate force arriving from the northeast on the Harrisburg Road (near flagpole, a mile eastward). As the Union troops north of Gettysburg retreated, the men on this ridge became isolated and withdrew to Cemetery Hill, south of the town.

The large white building on this side of Gettysburg is "Old Dorm" at Gettysburg College, used as a hospital during the battle. Beyond the town is Culp's Hill (see the observation tower), and in the right background is Cemetery Hill.

STOP 4. SEMINARY RIDGE

(North Carolina Monument.)

General Lee had failed to achieve any definite gains July 2 against the Union left flank at Little Round Top and the Peach Orchard, or the right flank at Spangler's Spring and Culp's Hill. He therefore marshaled his forces on the forenoon of July 3 for a final thrust against the center of the Union line on Cemetery Ridge. For nearly 2 hours, 138 Confederate guns on this ridge directed a heavy fire at the Union positions. Lee then sent 15,000 men across the open ground with the Copse of Trees (No. 8 on the Tour Map) as their objective. Spearheaded by Pickett's division, and therefore known as Pickett's Charge, this famous attack failed to break the strong Union positions at the stone wall. The advance marked the end of battle and the failure has been called the High Water Mark of the Confederacy. Lee gave up hope of further attack on this field, and on the following day began his retreat toward the Potomac and Virginia.

The wooded knoll to the east is Cemetery Hill (No. 10 on the Tour Map). Cemetery Ridge extends southward to Little Round Top (No. 7 on the Tour Map), the small hill partially cleared of trees at the left of Big Round Top. The Copse of Trees and The Angle (No. 8 on the Tour Map) are on the crest of the Cemetery Ridge where the flagpole appears.

STOP 5. WARFIELD RIDGE

The Union General Sickles, at noon July 2, began moving his troops forward from Cemetery Ridge and Little Round Top to Devil's Den Ridge and the Peach Orchard. Longstreet's Confederate corps was already marching from the Chambersburg Road to extend the line southward across the Emmitsburg Road. At 3:30 p. m., as Sickles' men were taking position at the Peach Orchard and the Emmitsburg Road, a half-mile north of here, Longstreet brought his army into position on this ridge. A brisk artillery exchange opened. Longstreet directed his infantry attack first at Little Round Top (the partially cleared hill to your right) and then along the whole Union line northward to the Peach Orchard and the Emmitsburg Road. Four hours later, as darkness gathered, the Union line had been shattered and forced to retreat. The Confederates gained possession of the west slope of Big Round Top, Devil's Den, and the high ground in the vicinity of the Peach Orchard.

STOP 6. DEVIL'S DEN

When General Sickles moved his corps forward to the Peach Orchard and the Emmitsburg Road at 3 p. m., his left flank was here at Devil's Den. Longstreet's Confederate brigades soon came charging from the west. Striking the entire Union line, the base of Little Round Top and this area quickly became a shambles. After hours of desperate struggle, the Union line had been broken and the remnants forced to the rear. The Confederates were now in possession of the west slope of Big Round Top, Devil's Den, the Wheatfield, and the Peach Orchard. Sharpshooters, using the large boulders as defense positions, fired at Union men on the crest of Little Round Top, 700 yards distant. A typical sharpshooter's barricade may still be seen at the top of Devil's Den.

STOP 7. LITTLE ROUND TOP

As Sickles completed the forward movement from Little Round Top and the area northward, his new line extended from the Peach Orchard southeastward through the Wheatfield to Devil's Den (see boulders below). Longstreet's attack on Little Round Top developed from the ridge a mile westward. His brigades successively struck the entire Union line from Devil's Den to the Emmitsburg Road. The Confederates in a 4-hour fight broke the entire Union line, and the remnants of Sickles' corps were forced to retreat to the rear of the Round Tops. The Confederates gained possession of the west slope of Big Round Top, Devil's Den, the Wheatfield (the open ground surrounded by woods), and the Peach Orchard (near the white buildings on the ridge). The quick action of General Warren (see bronze figure to the north) in bringing troops to Little Round Top saved the hill for the Union. The stone breastworks on the slope of the hill were constructed during the night of July 2 as a defense measure against further attack. Big Round Top, a quarter of a mile southward, was heavily wooded at the time of the battle and could not be used to advantage by either artillery or infantry.

STOP 8. CEMETERY RIDGE (THE ANGLE)

On the afternoon of July 2, General Lee had tried to turn the left flank of the Union line at Little Round Top and the Peach Orchard, and the right flank at Culp's Hill and Spangler's Spring. Meeting with only partial success in these attempts, he then planned to strike the center. First he massed his artillery on Seminary Ridge and across the fields. Many batteries were hardly more than 800 yards west of here. Beginning at 1 o'clock they engaged in an artillery duel of nearly 2 hours with the powerful Union batteries on this ridge. Then 15,000 men, in a battle line a mile in length, and spearheaded by Pickett's division, started from the Confederate lines across the open fields, with the Copse of Trees as their guide. When they reached the Emmitsburg Road 300 yards away, the men charged. Canister from Union artillery and concentrated infantry fire from the Union men at the stone walls soon cut wide gaps in the Confederate line. They reached the wall, and a small band of men crossed, but the tide had turned. In Lee's final great effort, he had lost nearly 10,000 of his men. The remnants gave way and soon were in full retreat to the Confederate lines. The counterattack, which Lee feared, never developed.

The Copse of Trees is at your left, surrounded by the iron fence. The position of Cushing's battery of United States artillery, which held the position at The Angle, is marked by four guns. The statue of General Meade stands to the right and rear.

STOP 9. MEADE'S HEADQUARTERS

Gen. George G. Meade, commanding the Union Army, arrived on the field near midnight, July 1. He used the Leister house as his headquarters.

On the night of July 2, General Meade called a council of his corps commanders in this house to determine whether they should hold the positions then established. The commanders advised him to hold the existing lines. Meade, agreeing with their advice and expecting the next attack on the center of his line, began the concentration of artillery and infantry strength in this area.

The Leister house and barn were badly damaged by the artillery fire which preceded Pickett's Charge.

STOP 10. NATIONAL CEMETERY

Soon after the battle, Governor Curtin, of Pennsylvania, commissioned Attorney David Wills, of Gettysburg, to purchase this ground as a cemetery for the Union dead. While reburials from the temporary graves on the battlefield were in progress, a committee arranged for a formal dedication on November 19, 1863. President Lincoln delivered his famous Gettysburg Address on that occasion. The National Monument, commemorating the Union soldiers who fell at Gettysburg, was dedicated, in 1869, on the site where Lincoln spoke. A memorial to the address was erected, in 1912, near the west gate of the cemetery.

STOP 11. CYCLORAMA OF PICKETT'S CHARGE

The Cyclorama of Pickett's Charge is regarded as a masterpiece of art. It offers an unsurpassed picture of the wartime appearance of the field, the manner of fighting, and of equipment employed. This magnificent painting, measuring 370 feet in circumference and 30 feet in height, was acquired by the National Park Service in 1942. The French artist, Paul Philippoteaux, completed the painting in 1884. It was brought to Gettysburg in 1913 when it was first mounted and exhibited in connection with the observance of the 50th anniversary of the Battle of Gettysburg.

STOP 12. EAST CEMETERY HILL

Early's Confederates assaulted Union positions here at dusk on July 2, in coordination with an attack on Culp's Hill (to your right). Rodes' men failed to charge from the west at the same time. Early's troops took possession of the hill and many of the guns, but in the absence of support from Rodes they were driven back. The desperate hand-to-hand fighting lasted long after dark.

Culp's Hill is one-quarter mile eastward (see the observation tower) and Spangler's Spring a few hundred yards beyond. Oak Ridge, a landmark of the first day's battle, appears northwest of the town.

STOP 13. CULP'S HILL

A Confederate attack was directed against this hill on July 2 in conjunction with the assault on East Cemetery Hill. Because of the steep incline and the strength of the Union positions here at the crest, the

Confederate force shifted southward across Rock Creek for a flank attack. Most of the Union troops had been ordered earlier to the defense of the Wheatfield and Peach Orchard. The Confederates, meeting with little resistance, took possession of the Union earthworks on the south slope of this hill. Before a Confederate attack developed against this position on the following morning, the Union force had returned. After fighting throughout the forenoon of July 3, they forced the Confederates out of the Union defense works. The Union brigade commanded by General Greene retained this position throughout the battle of July 2 and 3.

STOP 14. SPANGLER'S SPRING

Failing to take possession of Culp's Hill on the evening of July 2, Johnson's Confederate force shifted southward across Rock Creek and attacked the Union position on the hill north of this spring. The defense works here had been vacated an hour earlier when most of the troops were called to help defend the Union line in the Wheatfield and Peach Orchard. The Confederates then took possession of the Union works. The Union forces, having returned during the night, opened fire at dawn on July 3 with artillery and infantry. Confederate troops who were posted in the Union works and in rear of the stone wall on the hill to the north made a determined stand. After hard fighting, which ended only at noon, the Union force succeeded in driving the Confederates out of these works and eastward beyond striking range.

The Park

In 1895, the battlefield was established by act of Congress as Gettysburg National Military Park. In that year, the Gettysburg Battlefield Memorial Association, which had been founded April 30, 1864, for the purpose of commemorating "the great deeds of valor, endurance, and noble self-sacrifice, and to perpetuate the memory of the heroes, and the signal events which render these battlegrounds illustrious," transferred its holdings of 600 acres of land, 17 miles of avenues, and 320 monuments and markers to the Federal Government. Under the jurisdiction of the War Department until 1933, the park was transferred in that year to the Department of the Interior to be administered by the National Park Service. Today, the park consists of 2,554.82 acres of land and 26 miles of paved roads.

The fields over which the battles were fought cover about 16,000 acres and include the town of Gettysburg. A total of 2,390 monuments, tablets, and markers have been erected over the years to indicate the positions where infantry, artillery, and cavalry units fought. Of the 354 Union and 272 Confederate cannon engaged or held in reserve during the battle, 233 Federal and 182 Confederate are located on the field in the approximate position of the batteries during the battle.

Anniversary Reunions of the Civil War Veterans

The great interest of veterans and the public alike in the Gettysburg battlefield has been reflected over the years in three outstanding anniversary celebrations. Dominant in the observance of the 25th anniversary in 1888 were the veterans themselves, who returned to encamp on familiar ground. It was on this occasion that a large number of regimental monuments, erected by survivors of regiments or by States, were dedicated. Again, in 1913, on the 50th anniversary, even though the ranks were gradually thinning, the reunion brought thousands of veterans back to the battlefield. Perhaps the most impressive tribute to the surviving veterans occurred July 1-4, 1938, on the occasion of the observance of the 75th anniversary of the battle and the last reunion of the men who wore the blue and the gray. Although 94 years was the average age of those attending, 1,845 veterans, out of a total of about 8,000 then living, returned for the encampment. It was on this occasion that the Eternal Light Peace Memorial was dedicated.

How to Reach the Park

Gettysburg National Military Park and National Cemetery are accessible by highway over U. S. No. 30 from the east and west, U. S. No. 15 from the north and south; U. S. No. 140 from Baltimore, Md.; State No. 34 from Carlisle, Pa.; and State No. 116 from Hagerstown, Md., and Hanover, Pa. Greyhound Bus Lines operate over U. S. Nos. 30 and 140; the Blue Ridge Lines over U. S. No. 15 from the south; and the Gettysburg-Harrisburg Bus Line over U. S. No. 15 from Harrisburg.

Administration

Gettysburg National Military Park is administered by the National Park Service of the United States Department of the Interior. Communications should be addressed to the Superintendent, Gettysburg National Military Park, Gettysburg, Pa.

Related Areas

Significant parts of most of the major battlefields of the Civil War have been set aside under the control of the Federal Government to be administered as national military areas by the National Park Service. Among the areas in this group are: Antietam National Battlefield Site, Md.; Manassas National Battlefield Park, Va.; Fredericksburg and Spotsylvania County Battlefields Memorial National Military Park (includes Chancellorsville, The Wilderness, Spotsylvania Court House, and Fredericksburg battlefields), Va.; Petersburg National Military Park, Va.; Richmond National Battlefield Park, Va.; Appomattox Court House National Historical Park, Va.; Shiloh National Military Park, Tenn; Fort Donelson National Military Park, Tenn.; Stones River National Military Park, Tenn.; Chickamauga and Chattanooga National Military Park, Tenn.-Ga.; Kennesaw Mountain National Battlefield Park, Ga.; Fort Sumter National Monument, S. C.; Vicksburg National Military Park, Miss.; and Fort Pulaski National Monument, Ga.

Visitor Facilities

Information and free literature concerning the park may be obtained at the National Park Service museum in the Post Office building, at the national cemetery office, and at the park entrance stations. The services of park historians are available free for explanation of the battle, talks over a relief model of the battlefield in the museum, and for field tours with educational groups. A historian is stationed at Little Round Top during the summer season.

Field exhibits, consisting of a map of the battlefield and wartime photographs, are located at important points in the park for the use and interest of the public. With the exception of December, January, and February, the cyclorama is open weekdays from 10 a. m. to 12 noon and 1 p. m. to 5 p. m. and on Sundays 10 a. m. to 12 noon and 1 p. m. to 6 p. m. The admission fee is 25 cents for persons 12 years of age and over. School groups, 12 to 18 years of age, and children under 12 years of age are admitted free. Battlefield guides, licensed by the National Park Service, operate under the supervision of the park superintendent. A complete tour of the park, which covers the battleground of July 1, north and west of Gettysburg, and of July 2 and 3, south of the town, requires approximately 2 hours, and the guide fee is $4. A special tour, covering the main points of interest and requiring about 1 hour, is available at a fee of $3. The guide fee for a short bus tour is $5; for a long bus tour $6.

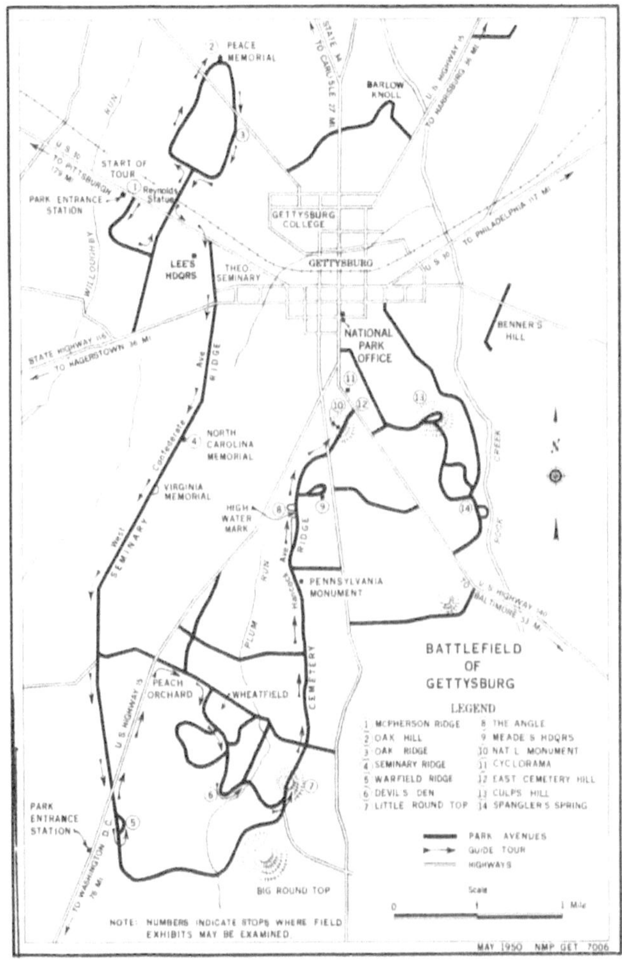

BATTLEFIELD OF GETTYSBURG

LEGEND

1 MCPHERSON RIDGE
2 OAK HILL
3 OAK RIDGE
4 SEMINARY RIDGE
5 WARFIELD RIDGE
6 DEVIL'S DEN
7 LITTLE ROUND TOP
8 THE ANGLE

9 MEADE'S HDQRS.
10 NAT'L. MONUMENT
11 CYCLORAMA
12 EAST CEMETERY HILL
13 CULPS HILL
14 SPANGLER'S SPRING

NATIONAL PARK SERVICE
HISTORICAL HANDBOOK SERIES

(Price lists of National Park Service publications may be obtained from
the Superintendent of Documents,
Washington 25, D.C.)

Antietam
Bandelier
Chalmette
Chickamauga and Chattanooga Battlefields
Custer Battlefield
Custis-Lee Mansion, the Robert E. Lee Memorial
Fort Laramie
Fort McHenry
Fort Necessity
Fort Pulaski
Fort Raleigh
Fort Sumter
George Washington Birthplace
Gettysburg
Guilford Courthouse
Hopewell Village
Independence
Jamestown, Virginia
Kings Mountain
The Lincoln Museum and the House Where Lincoln Died
Manassas (Bull Run)
Montezuma Castle
Morristown, a Military Capital of the Revolution
Ocmulgee
Petersburg Battlefields
Saratoga
Scotts Bluff
Shiloh
Statue of Liberty
Vanderbilt Mansion
Vicksburg
Yorktown